Dec. 2018

Dear Emily,

Enjoy baking!
Make sure you share
with me :)

Merry Christmas,
Aunty Elena

# Monkey
# BREADS
## AND MORE

Publications International, Ltd.

Photography on pages 5, 7, 11, 13, 17, 21, 23, 25, 27, 29, 31, 33, 35, 41, 49, 53, 57 and 59 by PIL Photo Studio North.

**Pictured on the front cover:** Cinnamini Monkey Bread *(page 20)*.

**Pictured on the back cover** *(left to right):* S'more Monkey Bread *(page 16)*, Pull-Apart Garlic Cheese Bread *(page 52)* and Chocolate-Stuffed Doughnuts *(page 112)*.

ISBN: 978-1-68022-066-7

Library of Congress Control Number: 2015933674

Manufactured in China.

8 7 6 5 4 3 2 1

**Microwave Cooking:** Microwave ovens vary in wattage. Use the cooking times as guidelines and check for doneness before adding more time.

Publications International, Ltd.

# Table of
## CONTENTS

# Monkey
## — ∞ —
## BREADS

## Cookie Dough Monkey Bread

### MAKES ABOUT 16 SERVINGS

1 package (about 16 ounces) break-apart
   refrigerated chocolate chip cookie dough
   (24 cookies)

2 packages (7½ ounces each) refrigerated
   buttermilk biscuits (10 biscuits per package)
1 cup semisweet chocolate chips, divided
¼ cup whipping cream

**1.** Preheat oven to 350°F. Generously spray 12-cup (10-inch) bundt pan with nonstick cooking spray.

**2.** Break cookie dough into 24 pieces; split each piece in half to make 48 pieces. Separate biscuits; cut each biscuit into four pieces with scissors. Layer half of cookie dough and half of biscuit pieces in prepared pan, alternating doughs. Sprinkle with ¼ cup chocolate chips. Repeat layers with remaining cookie dough and biscuit pieces; sprinkle with ¼ cup chocolate chips.

**3.** Bake 27 to 30 minutes or until biscuits are golden brown, covering pan loosely with foil during last 10 minutes of baking. Remove pan to wire rack; let stand, covered, 5 minutes. Loosen edges of bread with knife; invert onto serving plate.

**4.** Pour cream into medium microwavable bowl; microwave on HIGH 1 minute or until boiling. Add remaining ½ cup chocolate chips; stir until chocolate is melted. Let stand 5 minutes to thicken slightly. Drizzle glaze over monkey bread.

# Spicy Pepperoni Pizza Monkey Bread

MAKES 12 SERVINGS

2 tablespoons olive oil

1 package (about 4 ounces) pepperoni slices, chopped (¼-inch pieces)

1 clove garlic, minced

⅛ teaspoon red pepper flakes

¼ cup chopped fresh parsley

3 tablespoons butter, melted

1 cup shredded Parmesan cheese

1 loaf (1 pound) frozen pizza dough, thawed according to package directions

Marinara sauce, heated, for dipping (optional)

**1.** Spray 12-cup (10-inch) bundt pan with nonstick cooking spray.

**2.** Heat oil in large skillet over medium heat. Add pepperoni, cook and stir 5 minutes. Add garlic and red pepper flakes; cook and stir 3 minutes. Remove to medium bowl; stir in parsley and butter until blended. Stir in cheese.

**3.** Roll 1-inch pieces of dough into balls. Roll balls in pepperoni mixture to coat; layer in prepared pan. Cover and let rise about 45 minutes or until doubled in size. Preheat oven to 375°F.

**4.** Bake 30 to 35 minutes or until golden brown. Cool in pan on wire rack 5 minutes. Loosen edges of bread with knife; invert onto serving plate. Serve warm with marinara sauce, if desired.

# Cinnamon Coffee Monkey Bread

### MAKES 12 SERVINGS

½ cup sugar

1 tablespoon ground cinnamon

1 tablespoon instant coffee granules

3 packages (7½ ounces each) refrigerated buttermilk biscuits (10 biscuits per package)

Cinnamon Coffee Glaze (recipe follows)

**1.** Preheat oven to 350°F. Spray 12-cup (10-inch) bundt pan with nonstick cooking spray.

**2.** Combine sugar, cinnamon and instant coffee in small bowl; mix well.

**3.** Separate biscuits; cut each biscuit into four pieces with scissors. Roll each piece into a ball; roll balls in sugar mixture to coat. Layer in prepared pan.

**4.** Bake 30 minutes or until golden brown. Cool in pan on wire rack 5 minutes. Loosen edges of bread with knife; invert onto serving plate.

**5.** Prepare Cinnamon Coffee Glaze; drizzle over monkey bread. Serve warm.

## Cinnamon Coffee Glaze

½ cup (1 stick) butter

1 cup packed brown sugar

2 tablespoons ground cinnamon

1 teaspoon instant coffee granules

Combine butter, brown sugar, cinnamon and instant coffee in small saucepan; cook and stir over medium-low heat about 2 minutes or until brown sugar is dissolved and glaze is smooth.

# Breakfast Sausage Monkey Muffins

## MAKES 12 MUFFINS

12 ounces bulk pork sausage

1 egg, beaten

1½ cups (6 ounces) shredded Mexican cheese blend, divided

2 packages (7½ ounces each) refrigerated buttermilk biscuits (10 biscuits per package)

1. Preheat oven to 350°F. Spray 12 standard (2½-inch) muffin cups with nonstick cooking spray.

2. Cook and stir sausage in large skillet over medium-high heat about 8 minutes or until no longer pink, breaking apart any large pieces. Spoon sausage and drippings into large bowl; let cool 2 minutes. Add egg; stir until blended. Stir in 1¼ cups cheese.

3. Separate biscuits; cut each biscuit into four pieces with scissors. Roll biscuit pieces in sausage mixture to coat; place six to seven pieces in each muffin cup. Sprinkle with remaining ¼ cup cheese.

4. Bake about 22 minutes or until golden brown. Remove muffins to paper towel-lined plate. Serve warm.

# Cranberry Brie Bubble Bread

### MAKES 12 SERVINGS

3 cups all-purpose flour

1 package (¼ ounce) rapid-rise active dry yeast

1 teaspoon salt

1 cup warm water (120°F)

¼ cup (½ stick) plus 2 tablespoons butter, melted, divided

¾ cup finely chopped pecans or walnuts

¼ cup packed brown sugar

¼ teaspoon coarse salt

1 package (7 ounces) Brie cheese, cut into ¼-inch pieces

1 cup whole berry cranberry sauce

**1.** Combine flour, yeast and 1 teaspoon salt in large bowl of stand mixer. Stir in water and 2 tablespoons melted butter to form rough dough. Knead with dough hook at low speed 5 to 7 minutes or until dough is smooth and elastic.

**2.** Shape dough into a ball. Place in greased bowl; turn to grease top. Cover and let rise in warm place about 45 minutes or until doubled in size.

**3.** Spray 2-quart ovenproof bowl or baking dish with nonstick cooking spray. Combine pecans, brown sugar and coarse salt in shallow bowl. Place remaining ¼ cup melted butter in another shallow bowl. Turn out dough onto lightly floured surface; pat and stretch into 9×6-inch rectangle. Cut dough into 1-inch pieces; roll into balls.

**4.** Dip balls of dough in butter; roll in pecan mixture to coat. Place in prepared baking dish, layering with cheese and spoonfuls of cranberry sauce. Cover and let rise in warm place about 45 minutes or until dough is puffy. Preheat oven to 350°F.

**5.** Bake 30 minutes or until dough is firm and filling is bubbly. Cool on wire rack 15 to 20 minutes. Serve warm.

# Bacon Cheddar Monkey Bread

### MAKES 12 SERVINGS

1¾ cups (7 ounces) shredded sharp Cheddar cheese

12 ounces bacon, cooked and chopped (about 1 cup)

¼ cup finely chopped green onions

2¾ to 3 cups all-purpose flour, divided

1 package (¼ ounce) rapid-rise active dry yeast

1 teaspoon salt

1 cup warm water (120°F)

2 tablespoons olive oil

⅓ cup butter, melted

1 egg

**1.** Combine cheese, bacon and green onions in medium bowl; mix well.

**2.** Combine 1½ cups flour, yeast, and salt in large bowl of stand mixer; stir to combine. Add water and oil; beat with paddle attachment at medium speed 3 minutes.

**3.** Replace paddle attachment with dough hook; beat in 1¼ cups flour until dough comes together. Add 1 cup cheese mixture; knead at medium-low speed 6 to 8 minutes or until dough is smooth and elastic, adding remaining ¼ cup flour if necessary to clean side of bowl. Place dough in greased bowl; turn to grease top. Cover and let rise in warm place about 30 minutes or until doubled in size.

**4.** Generously spray 12-cup (10-inch) bundt pan with nonstick cooking spray. Whisk butter and egg in shallow bowl until blended. Punch down dough. Roll 1-inch pieces of dough into balls. Dip balls in butter mixture; roll in remaining cheese mixture to coat. Layer in prepared pan. Cover and let rise in warm place about 40 minutes or until almost doubled in size. Preheat oven to 375°F.

**5.** Bake about 35 minutes or until golden brown. Loosen edges of bread with knife; invert onto wire rack. Cool 5 minutes; serve warm.

# S'more Monkey Bread

## MAKES 5 SERVINGS

¼ cup graham cracker crumbs

¼ cup packed brown sugar

2 tablespoons butter, melted

1 package (7½ ounces) refrigerated buttermilk biscuits (10 biscuits)

¼ cup milk chocolate chips

¾ cup mini marshmallows

**1.** Preheat oven to 350°F. Spray five 4-ounce ramekins or custard cups with nonstick cooking spray.

**2.** Combine graham cracker crumbs and brown sugar in medium bowl. Place butter in small bowl.

**3.** Separate biscuits; cut each biscuit into four pieces with scissors. Dip four biscuit pieces in butter; roll in crumb mixture to coat. Place in one prepared ramekin; sprinkle with about seven chocolate chips and seven marshmallows, pressing chips into biscuit dough. Dip four more biscuit pieces in butter; roll in crumb mixture to coat. Place pieces over bottom layer in ramekin; top with chocolate chips and marshmallows. Repeat with remaining ingredients and ramekins. Place ramekins on baking sheet.

**4.** Bake about 18 minutes or until golden brown. Serve warm.

**VARIATION:** To use a muffin pan instead of ramekins, double all ingredients. Spray 11 standard (2½-inch) muffin pan cups with nonstick cooking spray. Use seven biscuit pieces in each muffin cup, layering with chocolate chips and mini marshmallows as directed in step 3. Bake as directed above. Loosen edges of muffins with knife immediately after baking; remove muffins to serving plate. Makes 11 muffins.

# Mexican Monkey Bread

### MAKES 10 SERVINGS

½ cup (1 stick) butter, melted

2 tablespoons chili powder

1 tablespoon ground cumin

2 packages (about 16 ounces each) frozen bread dough, thawed and cut into 1-inch cubes

2 cups (8 ounces) shredded Monterey Jack or Mexican blend cheese, divided

2 cups FRENCH'S® French Fried Onions, divided

1 can (4½ ounces) chopped green chilies, drained

**1.** Grease bottom and side of 10-inch tube pan. Combine melted butter and spices in small bowl. Dip bread cubes, one at a time, into butter mixture. Place ⅓ of bread cubes in bottom of prepared pan.

**2.** Sprinkle with ⅔ cup cheese, ⅔ cup French Fried Onions and half of chilies. Repeat layers. Top with remaining ⅓ of bread cubes. Cover pan with plastic wrap and place on baking sheet. Let rest in draft-free place for 1 hour or until doubled in size.

**3.** Preheat oven to 375°F. Bake 35 minutes or until golden. Sprinkle with remaining cheese and onions; bake 5 minutes or until cheese melts and onions are golden. Loosen edges of bread; invert onto baking rack. Immediately invert onto serving platter. Serve warm.

**PREP TIME:** 15 minutes
**STAND TIME:** 1 hour
**BAKE TIME:** 40 minutes

# Cinnamini Monkey Bread

## MAKES ABOUT 16 SERVINGS

3 cups all-purpose flour

1 package (¼ ounce) rapid-rise active dry yeast

1 teaspoon salt

1 cup warm water (120°F)

2 tablespoons butter, melted

5 tablespoons butter, very soft, divided

½ cup packed brown sugar

2 teaspoons ground cinnamon

¼ teaspoon coarse salt

1 cup powdered sugar

2 ounces cream cheese, softened

3 tablespoons milk

**1.** Combine flour, yeast and 1 teaspoon salt in large bowl of stand mixer. Stir in water and 2 tablespoons melted butter to form rough dough. Knead with dough hook at low speed 5 to 7 minutes or until dough is smooth and elastic.

**2.** Shape dough into a ball. Place in greased bowl; turn to grease top. Cover and let rise in warm place about 1 hour or until doubled in size.

**3.** Grease 12-cup (10-inch) bundt pan with 1 tablespoon soft butter. Combine brown sugar, cinnamon and coarse salt in shallow bowl. Turn out dough onto lightly floured surface. Roll dough into 24×16-inch rectangle. Cut lengthwise into four 24×4-inch strips.

**4.** Spread 1 tablespoon softened butter over each dough strip; sprinkle evenly with cinnamon-sugar, pressing gently to adhere. Starting with long side, roll up dough jelly-roll style; pinch seam to seal. Cut crosswise into 1-inch slices; layer slices in prepared pan, placing cut sides of slices against side of pan. Cover and let rise in warm place 30 minutes or until dough is puffy. Preheat oven to 350°F.

**5.** Bake 20 to 25 minutes or until bread is firm and lightly browned. Loosen edges of bread with knife; immediately invert onto serving plate. Cool slightly.

**6.** Whisk powdered sugar, cream cheese and milk in medium bowl until smooth. Drizzle over bread. Serve warm.

# Apple Pie Monkey Bread

MAKES ABOUT 12 SERVINGS

½ cup (1 stick) butter, divided

2 large apples (1 pound), peeled and cut into ½-inch pieces (Fuji, Granny Smith or Braeburn)

½ cup plus 1 tablespoon sugar, divided

2½ teaspoons ground cinnamon, divided

2 packages (7½ ounces each) refrigerated buttermilk biscuits (10 biscuits per package)

½ cup finely chopped pecans

1. Preheat oven to 350°F. Spray 9-inch deep-dish pie plate with nonstick cooking spray.

2. Melt ¼ cup butter in large skillet or saucepan over medium heat. Add apples, 1 tablespoon sugar and ½ teaspoon cinnamon; cook and stir 5 minutes or until apples are tender and glazed. Transfer to large bowl. Melt remaining ¼ cup butter in same skillet, stirring to scrape up any glaze. Cool slightly.

3. Combine pecans, remaining ½ cup sugar and 2 teaspoons cinnamon in medium bowl. Separate biscuits; cut each biscuit into four pieces with scissors. Dip biscuit pieces in melted butter; roll in pecan mixture to coat. Place one quarter of biscuit pieces in prepared pie plate; top with one quarter of apples. Repeat layers three times. Sprinkle with remaining pecan mixture and drizzle with remaining butter.

4. Bake 30 minutes or until biscuits are firm and topping is golden brown. Serve warm.

# Mocha Monkey Bread

### MAKES 12 SERVINGS

DOUGH

- 3 cups all-purpose flour
- 3 tablespoons granulated sugar
- 1 tablespoon unsweetened cocoa powder
- 1 package (¼ ounce) rapid-rise active dry yeast
- 1½ teaspoons salt
- 1 teaspoon instant espresso powder
- 1 cup warm water (120°F)
- 2 tablespoons butter, melted

FILLING

- 5 tablespoons butter, melted, divided
- ¼ cup granulated sugar
- 1 tablespoon unsweetened cocoa powder
- 1 teaspoon instant espresso powder
- ¼ cup mini chocolate chips

GLAZE

- 1 cup powdered sugar
- 1 teaspoon instant espresso powder
- 1 to 2 tablespoons half-and-half
- 2 tablespoons mini chocolate chips

**1.** Combine flour, 3 tablespoons granulated sugar, 1 tablespoon cocoa, yeast, salt and 1 teaspoon espresso powder in large bowl of stand mixer. Stir in water and 2 tablespoons melted butter to form rough dough. Knead with dough hook at low speed 5 to 7 minutes or until dough is smooth and elastic.

**2.** Shape dough into a ball. Place in greased bowl; turn to grease top. Cover and let rise in warm place 30 to 45 minutes or until doubled in size.

**3.** Brush 12-cup (10-inch) bundt pan with 1 tablespoon melted butter. Place remaining 4 tablespoons butter in medium bowl. Combine ¼ cup granulated sugar, 1 tablespoon cocoa and 1 teaspoon espresso powder in small bowl. Turn dough out onto lightly floured surface; pat into 12×6-inch rectangle. Cut dough into 1-inch squares; shape into balls. Dip balls in butter; roll in sugar mixture to coat. Layer half of balls in prepared pan; sprinkle with ¼ cup mini chips. Top with remaining balls of dough. Cover and let rise in warm place about 30 minutes. Preheat oven to 350°F.

**4.** Bake about 25 minutes or until bread is firm and lightly browned. Loosen edges of bread with knife; immediately invert onto serving plate.

**5.** Combine powdered sugar and 1 teaspoon espresso powder in medium bowl. Stir in enough half-and-half to make thick, pourable glaze. Drizzle over bread; sprinkle with 2 tablespoons mini chips.

# Pretzel Monkey Bread

MAKES 12 SERVINGS

2½ cups all-purpose flour

1½ teaspoons rapid-rise active dry yeast

1 teaspoon sugar

¼ teaspoon salt

¾ cup warm water (120°F)

6 tablespoons butter, melted

½ cup baking soda

Coarse salt

6 tablespoons sour cream

2 tablespoons Dijon mustard

1 tablespoon honey

**1.** Combine flour, yeast, sugar and ¼ teaspoon salt in large bowl of stand mixer. Stir in ¾ cup water and 2 tablespoons melted butter to form rough dough. Knead with dough hook at low speed 5 to 7 minutes or until dough is smooth and elastic. Shape dough into a ball. Place in greased bowl; turn to grease top. Cover and let rise in warm place about 1 hour or until doubled in size.

**2.** Preheat oven to 400°F. Line baking sheet with foil; set aside. Brush 9-inch springform pan with 1 tablespoon butter. Spray outside of 6-ounce ramekin with nonstick cooking spray; place in center of pan. Turn out dough onto lightly floured surface; pat and stretch into 12×6-inch rectangle. Cut dough into 1-inch pieces.

**3.** Bring 12 cups water to a boil in large saucepan; add baking soda. Working in batches, add dough pieces to boiling water; cook 30 seconds and drain. Place half of hot dough pieces around ramekin in prepared pan; brush with half of remaining butter and sprinkle with coarse salt. Top with remaining dough pieces; brush with remaining butter and sprinkle with coarse salt. Place springform pan on prepared baking sheet.

**4.** Bake about 30 minutes or until pretzels are dark golden brown. Loosen edges of bread with knife; carefully remove side of pan.

**5.** For dipping sauce, combine sour cream, mustard and honey in small bowl. Carefully remove hot ramekin from center of pretzel ring and replace with bowl of sauce. (Ramekin from oven will be too hot for sauce.) Serve warm.

# Maple Bacon Monkey Bread

### MAKES 12 SERVINGS

10 slices bacon, cooked and coarsely chopped (about 12 ounces)

⅓ cup packed brown sugar

¼ teaspoon black pepper

3 tablespoons butter

3 tablespoons maple syrup

1 loaf (1 pound) frozen bread dough, thawed according to package directions

**1.** Spray 12-cup (10-inch) bundt pan with nonstick cooking spray.

**2.** Combine bacon, brown sugar and pepper in medium bowl. Combine butter and maple syrup in medium microwavable bowl; microwave on HIGH 30 seconds. Stir mixture; microwave 20 seconds or until butter is melted.

**3.** Roll 1-inch pieces of dough into balls. Dip balls in butter mixture; roll in bacon mixture to coat. Layer balls in prepared pan. Reheat any remaining butter mixture, if necessary; drizzle over top of dough. Cover and let rise in warm place about 45 minutes or until doubled in size. Preheat oven to 350°F.

**4.** Bake 30 to 35 minutes or until golden brown. Cool in pan on wire rack 5 minutes. Loosen edges of bread with knife; invert onto serving plate. Serve warm.

# Peanut Butter and Jelly Monkey Biscuits

MAKES 12 SERVINGS

¼ cup creamy peanut butter

2 tablespoons butter

2¼ cups all-purpose flour

¼ cup sugar

1 tablespoon baking powder

½ teaspoon salt

¼ cup (½ stick) cold butter, cut into pieces

¾ cup buttermilk

6 tablespoons seedless strawberry jam, or favorite flavor

**1.** Preheat oven to 350°F. Line 9×5-inch loaf pan with foil, leaving 2-inch overhang. Spray foil with nonstick cooking spray.

**2.** Combine peanut butter and 2 tablespoons butter in small saucepan; cook and stir over low heat until melted. Cool slightly.

**3.** Combine flour, sugar, baking powder and salt in medium bowl. Cut in cold butter with pastry blender or two knives until mixture resembles coarse crumbs. Stir in buttermilk just until moistened.

**4.** Turn out dough onto lightly floured surface. Knead six to eight times. Pat dough into 8×6-inch rectangle; cut into 1-inch squares. Roll one third of squares in peanut butter mixture to coat; place in single layer in prepared pan. Top with 2 tablespoons jam, dropping jam by small spoonfuls over dough. Repeat layers twice.

**5.** Bake 35 to 40 minutes or until jam is melted and bubbly and biscuits are flaky. Cool in pan on wire rack 10 minutes. Remove biscuits from pan using foil. Serve warm.

# Banana Monkey Bread

## MAKES 12 SERVINGS

2 ripe bananas

2 cups all-purpose flour, divided

¾ cup whole wheat flour

½ cup old-fashioned oats

¾ cup sugar, divided

¼ cup warm milk (120°F)

3 tablespoons vegetable or canola oil

1 package (¼ ounce) rapid-rise active dry yeast

1 teaspoon salt

2 teaspoons ground cinnamon, divided

5 tablespoons butter, melted, divided

**1.** Place bananas in large bowl of stand mixer. Beat with paddle attachment at low speed 1 minute or until bananas are mashed. Add ¼ cup all-purpose flour, whole wheat flour, oats, ¼ cup sugar, milk, oil, yeast, salt and 1 teaspoon cinnamon; beat at medium speed 3 minutes.

**2.** Replace paddle attachment with dough hook; beat in enough remaining all-purpose flour to form soft dough. Knead at low speed 5 minutes or until dough is smooth and elastic. Shape dough into a ball. Place in greased bowl; turn to grease top. Cover and let rise in warm place about 1 hour or until doubled in size.

**3.** Brush 12-cup (10-inch) bundt pan with 1 tablespoon butter. Place remaining 4 tablespoons butter in small bowl. Combine remaining ½ cup sugar and 1 teaspoon cinnamon in medium bowl. Turn out dough onto lightly floured surface; pat into 9-inch square. Cut into 1-inch squares; roll into balls. Dip balls in butter; roll in cinnamon-sugar to coat. Layer in prepared pan. Cover and let rise about 1 hour until dough is puffy. Preheat oven to 350°F.

**4.** Bake 30 minutes or until bread is firm and golden brown. Loosen edges of bread with knife; immediately invert onto serving plate. Cool slightly before serving.

# Pull-Apart
## ∞
# BREADS

## Olive Herb Pull-Aparts

### MAKES 10 SERVINGS

2½ tablespoons extra virgin olive oil, divided)

4 cloves garlic, minced

1 package (12 ounces refrigerated buttermilk biscuits (10 biscuits)

¼ teaspoon red pepper flakes

1 red onion, very thinly sliced

½ cup shredded or chopped fresh basil

½ (2¼-ounce) can sliced black olives, drained

2 teaspoons chopped fresh rosemary

1 ounce feta cheese, crumbled

**1.** Preheat oven to 400°F. Line large baking sheet with parchment paper.

**2.** Combine 1½ tablespoons oil and garlic in small bowl. Separate biscuits; place on prepared baking sheet about ½ inch apart.* Lightly spray with olive oil cooking spray; let stand 10 minutes.

**3.** Flatten biscuits. Sprinkle with red pepper flakes, gently pressing into biscuits. Brush with garlic oil; sprinkle with onions.

**4.** Combine basil, olives, rosemary and remaining 1 tablespoon oil in medium bowl; mix well. Spread mixture over biscuits; sprinkle with cheese.

**5.** Bake 10 minutes or until golden brown. Serve warm or at room temperature.

*For an attractive presentation, place 4 biscuits in a line down center of baking sheet. Arrange half of remaining biscuits on each side.*

# Cinnamon Pecan Rolls

MAKES 18 ROLLS

¼ cup (½ stick) butter, melted, divided

1 loaf (1 pound) frozen bread dough, thawed according to package directions

½ cup packed dark brown sugar

2 teaspoons ground cinnamon

½ cup chopped pecans

**1.** Brush large (10-inch) cast iron skillet with ½ tablespoon melted butter.

**2.** Roll out dough into 18×8-inch rectangle on lightly floured surface.

**3.** Combine brown sugar, 3 tablespoons butter and cinnamon in medium bowl; mix well. Brush mixture evenly over dough; sprinkle with pecans. Starting with long side, roll up tightly jelly-roll style. Pinch seam to seal.

**4.** Cut crosswise into 1-inch slices; place slices cut sides up in prepared skillet. Cover loosely and let rise in warm place about 30 minutes or until doubled in size. Preheat oven to 350°F.

**5.** Brush tops of rolls with remaining ½ tablespoon butter. Bake 20 to 25 minutes or until golden brown. Serve warm.

# Pesto Pull-Apart Swirls

## MAKES 24 SERVINGS

3 cups all-purpose flour, divided

1 package (¼ ounce) rapid-rise active dry yeast

1½ teaspoons salt

1 cup warm water (120°F)

2 tablespoons plus 2 teaspoons olive oil, divided

5 tablespoons shredded Parmesan cheese, divided

1 jar (4½ ounces) pesto sauce (about ¼ cup)

**1.** Combine flour, yeast and salt in large bowl of stand mixer. Stir in water and 2 tablespoons oil to form rough dough. Knead with dough hook at low speed 5 to 7 minutes or until dough is smooth and elastic.

**2.** Shape dough into a ball. Place in greased bowl; turn to grease top. Cover and let rise in warm place 30 to 45 minutes or until doubled in size.

**3.** Brush remaining 2 teaspoon oils on bottom and side of 8-inch round cake pan;* sprinkle with 2 tablespoons cheese. Turn out dough onto lightly floured surface; roll into 20×12-inch rectangle. Spread pesto over dough. Starting with long side, roll up dough jelly-roll style; pinch seam to seal. Stretch or roll dough until 24 inches in length. Cut crosswise into 1-inch slices; place 12 slices cut sides up in prepared pan. Sprinkle with 2 tablespoons cheese. Top with remaining 12 slices; sprinkle with remaining 1 tablespoon cheese. Cover and let rise in warm place 30 minutes. Preheat oven to 350°F.

**4.** Bake 20 minutes or until lightly browned. Invert onto wire rack; invert again onto serving plate and cool slightly. Serve warm.

*Use cake pan with sides at least 1½ inches high, preferably nonstick.*

# Prosciutto Provolone Pull-Apart Loaf

## MAKES 1 LOAF

12 frozen white dinner rolls (⅓ of 3-pound package),* thawed according to package directions

12 slices smoked provolone cheese (about 10 ounces)

4 ounces thinly sliced prosciutto

¼ cup (1 ounce) shredded Italian cheese blend

*If frozen dinner rolls are not available, substitute one 1-pound loaf of frozen bread dough or pizza dough. Thaw according to package directions and divide into 12 pieces.*

1. Spray 9×5-inch loaf pan with nonstick cooking spray.

2. Working with one roll at a time, press or stretch dough into 5-inch circle. Top with one slice provolone and one slice prosciutto, cutting prosciutto to fit as needed. Fold dough circle in half like a taco.

3. Stand prepared pan upright on short end; place dough semicircle in bottom of pan with round edge facing out. Repeat topping and folding with remaining rolls, provolone and prosciutto, stacking semicircles on top of each other in pan. Return pan to regular position with bottom on counter; cover and let rise in warm place about 40 minutes or until doubled in size. Preheat oven to 375°F. Sprinkle shredded cheese over top of loaf.

4. Bake 25 to 30 minutes or until golden brown. Cool in pan 5 minutes; remove to wire rack. Serve warm.

# Quick Chocolate Chip Sticky Buns

MAKES 8 STICKY BUNS

2 tablespoons butter

1 package (11 ounces) refrigerated French bread dough

¼ cup sugar

1 teaspoon ground cinnamon

½ cup mini semisweet chocolate chips

⅓ cup pecan pieces, toasted*

1 tablespoon maple syrup

*To toast pecans, spread in single layer on ungreased baking sheet. Bake in preheated 350°F oven 6 to 8 minutes or until golden brown, stirring frequently.

**1.** Preheat oven to 350°F. Place butter in 9-inch round cake pan; place pan in oven while preheating to melt butter.

**2.** Meanwhile, unroll dough on cutting board or clean work surface. Combine sugar and cinnamon in small bowl; sprinkle evenly over dough. Top with chocolate chips. Starting with short side, roll up dough jelly-roll style. Cut crosswise into 8 slices with serrated knife.

**3.** Remove pan from oven. Stir pecans and maple syrup into melted butter; mix well. Place slices cut sides up in pan, pressing gently into pecan mixture.

**4.** Bake 20 to 22 minutes or until golden brown. Immediately invert pan onto serving plate. Scrape any pecans or butter mixture remaining in pan over buns. Serve warm.

# Pull-Apart Rye Rolls

### MAKES 24 ROLLS

¾ cup water

2 tablespoons butter

2 tablespoons molasses

2¼ cups all-purpose flour, divided

½ cup rye flour

⅓ cup nonfat dry milk powder

1 package (¼ ounce) active dry yeast

1½ teaspoons salt

1½ teaspoons caraway seeds

Vegetable or olive oil

**1.** Combine water, butter and molasses in small saucepan; heat over low heat to 120°F. Combine 1¼ cups all-purpose flour, rye flour, milk powder, yeast, salt and caraway seeds in large bowl. Stir in water mixture with wooden spoon to form soft, sticky dough. Gradually add enough of remaining all-purpose flour to form rough dough.

**2.** Turn out dough onto lightly floured surface. Knead 5 to 8 minutes or until smooth and elastic, gradually adding remaining flour to prevent sticking, if necessary. Place in greased bowl; turn to grease top. Cover and let rise in warm place 35 to 40 minutes or until dough has increased in size by one third.

**3.** Spray 9-inch round cake pan with nonstick cooking spray. Punch down dough. Divide dough in half; roll each half into 12-inch log. Cut each log into 12 pieces with sharp knife; shape pieces into tight balls. Place in single layer in prepared pan. Brush tops with oil. Cover and let rise in warm place 45 minutes or until doubled in size. Preheat oven to 375°F.

**4.** Bake 15 to 20 minutes or until golden brown. Cool in pan on wire rack 5 minutes; remove to wire rack to cool completely.

# Cheddary Pull Apart Bread

### MAKES ABOUT 8 SERVINGS

1 round loaf corn or sourdough bread
(1 pound)*

½ cup (1 stick) butter or margarine, melted

¼ cup FRENCH'S® Classic Yellow® Mustard

½ teaspoon chili powder

½ teaspoon seasoned salt

¼ teaspoon garlic powder

1 cup (4 ounces) shredded Cheddar cheese

*You can substitute one 12-inch loaf of Italian bread for the corn bread.*

**1.** Cut bread into 1-inch slices, cutting about ⅔ of the way down through loaf. (Do not cut through bottom crust.) Turn bread ¼ turn and cut across slices in similar fashion.

**2.** Combine butter, mustard and seasonings in small bowl until blended. Brush cut surfaces of bread with butter mixture. Spread bread "sticks" apart and sprinkle cheese inside. Wrap loaf in foil.

**3.** Place packet on grid. Cook over medium coals about 30 minutes or until bread is toasted and cheese melts. Pull bread "sticks" apart to serve.

**PREP TIME:** 15 minutes
**COOK TIME:** 30 minutes

# Honey Butter Pull-Apart Bread

### MAKES 8 SERVINGS

3 cups all-purpose flour

1 package (¼ ounce) rapid-rise active dry yeast

1 teaspoon salt

1 cup warm water (120°F)

2 tablespoons butter, melted

¼ cup (½ stick) butter, softened

¼ cup honey

**1.** Combine flour, yeast and salt in large bowl of stand mixer. Stir in water and melted butter to form rough dough. Knead with dough hook at low speed 5 to 7 minutes or until dough is smooth and elastic.

**2.** Shape dough into a ball. Place in greased bowl; turn to grease top. Cover and let rise in warm place 45 minutes to an hour or until doubled in size.

**3.** Spray 8×4-inch loaf pan with nonstick cooking spray. Combine softened butter and honey in small bowl. Turn out dough onto lightly floured surface. Roll out dough into 18×10-inch rectangle; cut in half crosswise to make two 10×9-inch rectangles. Spread some of honey butter over one half of dough; top with remaining half. Cut dough in half crosswise to make two 9×5-inch rectangles. Spread some of honey butter over one half; top with remaining half. Cut dough in half lengthwise, then cut crosswise into 1-inch strips. Place rows of strips vertically in prepared pan. Cover and let rise in warm place 1 hour or until dough is puffy. Preheat oven to 350°F. Brush or dollop remaining honey butter over dough strips.

**4.** Bake 30 minutes or until bread is firm and golden brown. Immediately remove from pan to wire rack. Serve warm.

# Breakfast Biscuit Pull-Aparts

MAKES 8 SERVINGS

8 ounces bacon, chopped

1 small onion, finely chopped

1 clove garlic, minced

¼ teaspoon red pepper flakes

5 eggs

¼ cup milk

½ cup (2 ounces) shredded white Cheddar cheese, divided

¼ teaspoon salt

⅛ teaspoon ground black pepper

1 package (about 16 ounces) refrigerated jumbo buttermilk biscuits (8 biscuits)

**1.** Preheat oven to 425°F. Cook bacon in large (10-inch) cast iron skillet until crisp. Remove to paper towel-lined plate. Drain off and reserve drippings, leaving 1 tablespoon in skillet.

**2.** Add onion, garlic and red pepper flakes to skillet; cook and stir over medium heat about 8 minutes or until onion is very soft. Set aside to cool slightly.

**3.** Whisk eggs, milk, ¼ cup cheese, salt and black pepper in medium bowl until well blended. Stir in onion mixture.

**4.** Wipe out any onion mixture remaining in skillet; grease bottom and side of skillet with additional drippings, if necessary. Separate biscuits; arrange in single layer in bottom of skillet. (Bottom of skillet should be completely covered.) Pour egg mixture over biscuits; sprinkle with remaining ¼ cup cheese and cooked bacon.

**5.** Bake about 25 minutes or until puffed and golden brown. Serve warm.

# Pull-Apart Garlic Cheese Bread

### MAKES 12 SERVINGS

3 cups all-purpose flour

1 package (¼ ounce) rapid-rise active dry yeast

1 teaspoon salt

1 cup warm water (120°F)

2 tablespoons olive oil

6 cloves garlic, minced, divided

¼ cup (½ stick) butter

¼ teaspoon paprika

1 cup grated Parmesan cheese

1 cup (4 ounces) shredded mozzarella cheese

½ cup pizza sauce

Chopped fresh parsley (optional)

**1.** Combine flour, yeast and salt in large bowl of stand mixer. Stir in water and oil to form rough dough; add half of garlic. Knead with dough hook at low speed 5 to 7 minutes or until dough is smooth and elastic.

**2.** Shape dough into a ball. Place in greased bowl; turn to grease top. Cover and let rise in warm place 45 minutes to 1 hour or until doubled in size.

**3.** Melt butter in small skillet over medium-low heat. Add remaining garlic; cook and stir 1 minute. Stir in paprika; remove from heat. Brush 9-inch springform pan with some of butter mixture. Place 6-ounce ramekin in center of pan. Line baking sheet with foil. Place Parmesan in shallow bowl.

**4.** Turn out dough onto lightly floured surface; pat into 9-inch square. Cut dough into 1-inch squares; roll into balls. Dip half of balls in melted butter mixture; roll in Parmesan to coat. Place around ramekin in prepared pan; sprinkle with ½ cup mozzarella. Repeat with remaining dough and mozzarella. Cover and let rise in warm place 1 hour or until dough has risen to top of pan. Preheat oven to 350°F. Pour pizza sauce into ramekin. Place springform pan on prepared baking sheet.

**5.** Bake 20 to 25 minutes or until bread is firm and golden brown. Loosen edges of bread with knife; carefully remove side of pan. Sprinkle with parsley, if desired. Serve warm.

# Gooey Caramel and Chocolate Pecan Rolls

### MAKES 24 ROLLS

1 jar (12 ounces) caramel ice cream topping

⅔ cup coarsely chopped pecans

1 cup semisweet chocolate chips, divided

4 tablespoons butter, divided

2 loaves (1 pound each) frozen bread dough, thawed according to package directions

**1.** Divide caramel topping between two 9-inch round cake pans; spread in thin layer. Sprinkle pecans evenly over caramel.

**2.** Combine ⅔ cup chocolate chips and 2 tablespoons butter in medium microwavable bowl; microwave on HIGH 30 seconds. Stir; microwave at additional 20-second intervals until chocolate is melted and mixture is smooth.

**3.** Roll out one loaf of dough into 12×8-inch rectangle on lightly floured surface. Spread half of chocolate mixture over dough. Starting with long side, roll up dough jelly-roll style; pinch seam to seal. Cut crosswise into 12 (1-inch) slices; place slices cut sides up in one prepared pan. Repeat with remaining dough and chocolate mixture. Cover and let rise in warm place about 1 hour or until almost doubled in size. Preheat oven to 375°F.

**4.** Bake 20 to 25 minutes or until golden brown. Immediately invert onto serving plates.

**5.** Combine remaining ⅓ cup chocolate chips and 2 tablespoons butter in small bowl; microwave on HIGH 30 seconds. Stir; microwave at additional 20-second intervals until chocolate is melted and mixture is smooth. Drizzle over warm rolls.

# Spanikopita Pull-Aparts

## MAKES 24 ROLLS

4 tablespoons (½ stick) butter, melted, divided

12 frozen white dinner rolls (⅓ of 3-pound package),* thawed according to package directions

1 package (10 ounces) frozen chopped spinach, thawed and squeezed dry

4 green onions, finely chopped (about ¼ cup packed)

1 clove garlic, minced

1 teaspoon dried dill weed

½ teaspoon salt

⅛ teaspoon black pepper

1 cup (4 ounces) crumbled feta cheese

¾ cup (3 ounces) grated Monterey Jack cheese, divided

*If frozen dinner rolls are not available, substitute one 1-pound loaf of frozen bread dough or pizza dough. Thaw according to package directions and divide into 12 pieces.*

**1.** Brush large (10-inch) ovenproof skillet with ½ tablespoon melted butter. Cut rolls in half to make 24 balls of dough.

**2.** Combine spinach, green onions, garlic, dill, salt and pepper in medium bowl; mix well to break apart spinach. Add feta, ½ cup Monterey Jack and remaining 3½ tablespoons butter; mix well.

**3.** Coat each ball of dough with spinach mixture; arrange in single layer in prepared skillet. Sprinkle any remaining spinach mixture between and over balls of dough. Cover and let rise in warm place about 40 minutes or until almost doubled in size. Preheat oven to 350°F. Sprinkle with remaining ¼ cup Monterey Jack.

**4.** Bake 35 to 40 minutes or until golden brown. Serve warm.

# Super Simple Cheesy Bubble Loaf

### MAKES 12 SERVINGS

2 packages (7½ ounces each) refrigerated
buttermilk biscuits (10 biscuits per package)

2 tablespoons butter, melted
1½ cups (6 ounces) shredded Italian cheese blend

**1.** Preheat oven to 350°F. Spray 9×5-inch loaf pan with nonstick cooking spray.

**2.** Separate biscuits; cut each biscuit into four pieces with scissors. Layer half of biscuit pieces in prepared pan. Drizzle with 1 tablespoon butter; sprinkle with 1 cup cheese. Top with remaining biscuit pieces, 1 tablespoon butter and ½ cup cheese.

**3.** Bake about 25 minutes or until golden brown. Serve warm.

❧ TIP: It's easy to change up the flavors in this simple bread. Try Mexican cheese blend instead of Italian, and add taco seasoning and/or hot pepper sauce to the melted butter before drizzling it over the dough. Or, sprinkle ¼ cup chopped ham, salami or crumbled crisp-cooked bacon between the layers of dough.

# Cinnamon Raisin Rolls

## MAKES 18 ROLLS

1 package (16 ounces) hot roll mix,
    plus ingredients to prepare mix

⅓ cup raisins

4 tablespoons (½ stick) butter, softened,
    divided

¼ cup granulated sugar

2 teaspoons ground cinnamon

½ teaspoon ground nutmeg

1½ cups powdered sugar

1 to 2 tablespoons milk

½ teaspoon vanilla

**1.** Preheat oven to 375°F. Spray 13×9-inch baking pan with nonstick cooking spray.

**2.** Prepare hot roll mix according to package directions; stir in raisins. Knead dough on lightly floured surface about 5 minutes or until smooth and elastic. Cover dough with plastic wrap; let stand 5 minutes.

**3.** Roll out dough into 16×10-inch rectangle on floured surface. Spread with 2 tablespoons butter. Combine granulated sugar, cinnamon and nutmeg in small bowl; sprinkle evenly over dough. Starting with long side, roll up dough jelly-roll style; pinch seam to seal.

**4.** Gently stretch dough until 18 inches long. Cut crosswise into 1-inch slices; place slices cut sides up in prepared pan. Cover loosely and let rise 20 to 30 minutes or until doubled in size.

**5.** Bake 20 to 25 minutes or until golden brown. Cool in pan 3 minutes; remove to wire rack.

**6.** Combine powdered sugar, remaining 2 tablespoons butter, 1 tablespoon milk and vanilla in medium bowl; whisk until smooth. Add additional 1 tablespoon milk to thin glaze, if necessary. Spread glaze over warm rolls.

# Italian Pull-Apart Rolls

### MAKES 15 ROLLS

3¾ cups bread flour, divided

1½ tablespoons sugar

1 package (¼ ounce) rapid-rise active dry yeast

1½ teaspoons salt

¾ cup warm water (120°F)

½ cup warm milk (120°F)

2 tablespoons olive oil

¾ cup grated Parmesan cheese

2 teaspoons Italian seasoning

⅓ cup butter, melted

**1.** Combine 1½ cups flour, sugar, yeast and salt in large bowl of stand mixer. Add water, milk and oil; beat with paddle attachment at medium speed 3 minutes. Replace paddle attachment with dough hook; beat in enough remaining flour to form firm dough. Knead at medium-low speed 5 minutes. Place in greased bowl; turn to grease top. Cover and let rise in warm place about 30 minutes or until doubled in size.

**2.** Spray 2½-quart baking dish with nonstick cooking spray. Combine cheese and Italian seasoning in shallow bowl. Place melted butter in another shallow bowl.

**3.** Turn dough out onto lightly floured surface. Gently roll dough into 20-inch rope. Cut into 15 pieces; roll each piece into a ball. Dip balls in butter; roll in cheese mixture to coat. Place in prepared baking dish. Cover and let rise about 30 minutes or until doubled in size. Preheat oven to 375°F.

**4.** Bake about 30 minutes or until golden brown. Cool in pan on wire rack 10 minutes; invert onto serving plate. Serve warm.

# Rolls
# & BUNS

## Greek Spinach-Cheese Rolls

### MAKES 15 SERVINGS

1 package (1 pound) frozen bread dough, thawed according to package directions

1 package (10 ounces) frozen chopped spinach, thawed and squeezed dry

¾ cup (3 ounces) crumbled feta cheese

½ cup (2 ounces) shredded Monterey Jack cheese

4 green onions, thinly sliced

1 teaspoon dried dill weed

½ teaspoon garlic powder

½ teaspoon black pepper

**1.** Spray 15 standard (2½-inch) muffin cups with nonstick cooking spray. Roll out dough into 15×9-inch rectangle on lightly floured surface.

**2.** Combine spinach, feta, Monterey Jack, green onions, dill, garlic powder and pepper in large bowl; mix well. Spread spinach mixture evenly over dough to within 1 inch of long sides.

**3.** Starting with long side, tightly roll up dough jelly-roll style; pinch seam to seal. Place roll seam side down on work surface. Cut crosswise into 15 slices with serrated knife; place slices cut sides up in prepared muffin cups. Cover and let rise in warm place 30 minutes or until dough is slightly puffy. Preheat oven to 375°F.

**4.** Bake 20 to 25 minutes or until golden brown. Serve warm or at room temperature.

# Triple Chocolate Sticky Buns

MAKES 12 BUNS

### DOUGH

2⅔ cups bread flour

⅓ cup unsweetened cocoa powder

¼ cup granulated sugar

1 package (¼ ounce) rapid-rise active dry yeast

1 teaspoon salt

½ cup sour cream

1 egg

¼ cup warm water (120°F)

3 tablespoons butter, softened

### TOPPING

⅓ cup packed brown sugar

¼ cup (½ stick) butter

2 tablespoons light corn syrup

1 tablespoon unsweetened cocoa powder

### FILLING

⅓ cup packed brown sugar

½ teaspoon ground cinnamon

3 tablespoons butter, melted

⅔ cup chopped walnuts, toasted*

½ cup semisweet chocolate chips

*To toast walnuts, spread in single layer on baking sheet. Bake in preheated 350°F oven 6 to 8 minutes or until fragrant, stirring frequently.*

**1.** Combine flour, ⅓ cup cocoa, granulated sugar, yeast and salt in large bowl of stand mixer. Whisk sour cream and egg in small bowl until well blended. Add water, butter and sour cream mixture to flour mixture; beat with paddle attachment at medium speed 3 minutes.

**2.** Replace paddle attachment with dough hook; knead at medium-low speed about 6 minutes or until smooth. Place in greased bowl; turn to grease top. Cover and let rise in warm place about 40 minutes. (Dough will not double in size.)

**3.** Meanwhile, prepare topping and filling. Spray 9-inch round cake pan with nonstick cooking spray. Combine ⅓ cup brown sugar, ¼ cup butter, corn syrup and 1 tablespoon cocoa in small saucepan; heat over medium heat until brown sugar dissolves and mixture bubbles around edge, stirring frequently. Pour into prepared pan. Combine ¼ cup brown sugar and cinnamon in small bowl.

**4.** Roll out dough into 12×8-inch rectangle on lightly floured surface. Brush with melted butter and sprinkle with brown sugar mixture. Sprinkle with walnuts and chocolate chips; gently press filling into dough. Starting with long side, roll up tightly jelly-roll style; pinch seam to seal. Cut crosswise into 12 slices; place over topping in pan. Cover and let rise in warm place about 35 minutes or until doubled in size. Preheat oven to 375°F.

**5.** Bake about 25 minutes or just until buns in center of pan are firm to the touch. Immediately invert onto serving plate. Serve warm or at room temperature.

# Hawaiian Pizza Rolls

### MAKES 6 SERVINGS

2 tablespoons cornmeal, divided

1 package (about 14 ounces) refrigerated pizza dough

6 ounces thinly sliced Canadian bacon

⅓ cup crushed pineapple, drained

⅓ cup pizza sauce

3 pieces (1 ounce each) string cheese

**1.** Preheat oven to 400°F. Line baking sheet with parchment paper or spray with nonstick cooking spray. Sprinkle with 1 tablespoon cornmeal.

**2.** Roll out dough into 16½×11-inch rectangle on lightly floured surface. Sprinkle with remaining 1 tablespoon cornmeal. Cut into six squares. Top each square with bacon, pineapple and pizza sauce.

**3.** Cut each piece of string cheese in half. Place one piece of cheese in center of each square. Bring up two opposite sides of each square and seal. Place rolls seam side down on prepared baking sheet. Crimp ends of each roll to seal.

**4.** Bake 15 to 17 minutes or until golden brown. Remove to wire rack. Serve warm or at room temperature.

∞ TIP: Serve extra pizza sauce on the side for dipping.

# Ooey-Gooey Pineapple Buns >

MAKES 10 SERVINGS

⅔ cup packed brown sugar

¼ cup maple syrup

2 tablespoons butter, melted

1 teaspoon vanilla

1 can (8 ounces) pineapple tidbits, drained

½ cup chopped pecans

½ cup flaked coconut

1 package (12 ounces) refrigerated flaky biscuits (10 biscuits)

**1.** Preheat oven to 350°F.

**2.** Combine brown sugar, maple syrup, butter and vanilla in 11×7-inch baking dish; mix well. Sprinkle with pineapple, pecans and coconut.

**3.** Separate biscuits; cut each biscuit into four pieces with scissors. Place in single layer over coconut.

**4.** Bake 25 to 30 minutes or until deep golden brown. Invert onto serving plate; serve warm.

# Apple Butter Rolls

MAKES 12 SERVINGS

1 package (11 ounces) refrigerated breadstick dough (12 breadsticks)

2 tablespoons apple butter

¼ cup sifted powdered sugar

1 to 1½ teaspoons orange juice

¼ teaspoon grated orange peel (optional)

**1.** Preheat oven to 350°F. Line baking sheet with parchment paper or spray with nonstick cooking spray.

**2.** Unroll breadstick dough; separate into 12 pieces along perforations. Gently stretch each piece until 9 inches in length. Twist ends of each piece in opposite directions 3 to 4 times. Coil each twisted strip into snail shape on prepared baking sheet. Tuck ends underneath. Use thumb to make small indentation in center of each breadstick coil. Spoon about ½ teaspoon apple butter into each indentation.

**3.** Bake 11 to 13 minutes or until golden brown. Remove to wire rack to cool 10 minutes.

**4.** Combine powdered sugar and 1 teaspoon orange juice in small bowl; whisk until smooth. Add additional juice if necessary to make pourable glaze. Stir in orange peel, if desired. Drizzle glaze over rolls. Serve warm.

# Cinnamon Oat Rolls

### MAKES 9 ROLLS

1 pound frozen bread dough, thawed according to package directions

1 cup QUAKER® Oats (quick or old fashioned, uncooked)

⅓ cup firmly packed brown sugar

2 teaspoons ground cinnamon

⅓ cup (5 tablespoons plus 1 teaspoon) margarine or butter, melted

¾ cup raisins or dried cranberries

¼ cup orange marmalade

**1.** Let dough stand, covered, at room temperature 15 minutes to relax. Spray 8- or 9-inch square baking pan with nonstick cooking spray.

**2.** Combine oats, brown sugar and cinnamon in medium bowl. Add margarine; mix well. Stir in raisins. Set aside.

**3.** Roll dough into 12×10-inch rectangle. (Dough will be very elastic.) Spread evenly with oat mixture to within ½ inch of edges. Starting from long side, roll up; pinch seam to seal. With sharp knife, cut into 9 slices about 1¼ inches wide; place in prepared pan, cut sides down. Cover loosely with plastic wrap; let rise in warm place 30 minutes or until nearly doubled in size.

**4.** Heat oven to 350°F. Bake 30 to 35 minutes or until golden brown. Cool 5 minutes in pan on wire rack; remove from pan. Spread tops of rolls with marmalade. Serve warm.

# Baked Pork Buns

## MAKES 20 BUNS

1 tablespoon vegetable oil

2 cups coarsely chopped bok choy

1 small onion or large shallot, thinly sliced

1 container (18 ounces) refrigerated shredded barbecue pork

All-purpose flour

2 packages (10 ounces each) refrigerated jumbo buttermilk biscuits (5 biscuits per package)

**1.** Preheat oven to 350°F. Line baking sheet with parchment paper or spray with nonstick cooking spray.

**2.** Heat oil in large skillet over medium-high heat. Add bok choy and onion; cook and stir 8 to 10 minutes or until vegetables are tender. Remove from heat; stir in barbecue pork.

**3.** Lightly flour work surface. Separate biscuits; split each biscuit in half crosswise to create two thin biscuits. Roll each biscuit half into 5-inch circle.

**4.** Spoon heaping tablespoonful of pork mixture onto one side of each circle. Fold dough over filling to form semicircle; press edges to seal. Place buns on prepared baking sheet.

**5.** Bake 12 to 15 minutes or until golden brown. Serve warm.

# Quick Breakfast Rolls

MAKES 12 SERVINGS

¼ cup sliced almonds, toasted

½ cup packed brown sugar

1 teaspoon ground cinnamon

½ teaspoon ground nutmeg

4 tablespoons butter or margarine, divided

¾ cup DOLE® Frozen Mango Chunks, finely chopped, thawed, drained

1 package (8 ounces) refrigerated crescent rolls

1. Combine almonds, brown sugar, cinnamon and nutmeg in small bowl. Spray muffin pan with nonstick cooking spray.

2. Place 1 teaspoon butter and 1 tablespoon sugar mixture in each prepared muffin cup.

3. Add mango to remaining sugar mixture. Unroll crescent dough from package and pinch seams together. Spread mango mixture over dough. Roll up from long side. Cut into 12 pieces and place each spiral into a muffin cup.

4. Bake at 375°F 12 to 15 minutes. Loosen edges; invert pan onto baking sheet. Serve warm.

PREP TIME: 20 minutes
BAKE TIME: 15 minutes

# Dim Sum Chicken Buns

### MAKES 18 BUNS

6 to 8 dried shiitake mushrooms

3 green onions, minced

2 tablespoons prepared plum sauce

1 tablespoon hoisin sauce

2 teaspoons vegetable or peanut oil

8 ounces ground chicken

4 cloves garlic, minced

1 tablespoon minced fresh ginger

9 frozen dinner rolls, thawed according to package directions

1 egg, beaten

¾ teaspoon sesame seeds

1. Place mushrooms in small bowl. Cover with warm water; let stand 30 minutes. Line two baking sheets with parchment paper or spray with nonstick cooking spray.

2. Rinse mushrooms and drain, squeezing out excess water. Cut off and discard stems. Finely chop caps. Combine mushrooms, green onions, plum sauce and hoisin sauce in large bowl; mix well.

3. Heat oil in medium skillet over high heat. Add chicken; cook without stirring 1 to 2 minutes or until no longer pink. Add garlic and ginger; cook and stir 2 minutes. Stir in mushroom mixture.

4. Lightly flour hands and work surface. Cut rolls in half; roll each half into a ball. Shape each piece between hands to form disk. Press edge of disk between thumb and forefinger, working in circular motion to form circle 3 to 3½ inches in diameter (center of disk should be thicker than edges).

5. Place disks on work surface. Place 1 generous tablespoon filling in center of each disk. Lift edge of dough up and around filling; pinch together to seal. Place buns seam side down on prepared baking sheets. Cover with towel and let rise in warm place 45 minutes or until doubled in size. Preheat oven to 375°F. Brush buns with egg; sprinkle with sesame seeds.

6. Bake 16 to 18 minutes or until golden brown. Serve warm.

# Prosciutto Cheese Rolls

### MAKES 12 ROLLS

1 loaf (1 pound) frozen bread dough, thawed according to package directions

¼ cup garlic and herb spreadable cheese

6 thin slices prosciutto (3-ounce package)

6 slices (1 ounce each) provolone cheese

1. Spray 12 standard (2½-inch) muffin cups with nonstick cooking spray. Roll out dough into 12×10-inch rectangle on lightly floured surface.

2. Spread garlic and herb cheese evenly over dough. Arrange prosciutto slices over herb cheese; top with provolone slices. Starting with long side, roll up dough jelly-roll style; pinch seam to seal.

3. Cut crosswise into 1-inch slices; place slices cut sides up in prepared muffin cups. Cover and let rise in warm place 30 to 40 minutes or until nearly doubled in size. Preheat oven to 350°F.

4. Bake about 18 minutes or until golden brown. Loosen edges of rolls with knife; remove to wire rack. Serve warm.

# Mini Cinnamon Buns

### MAKES 24 MINI BUNS

2 tablespoons packed brown sugar

½ teaspoon ground cinnamon

1 package (8 ounces) refrigerated
   crescent roll dough

1 tablespoon butter, melted

½ cup powdered sugar

1 to 1½ tablespoons milk

**1.** Preheat oven to 375°F. Line baking sheet with parchment paper. Combine brown sugar and cinnamon in small bowl; mix well.

**2.** Unroll dough and separate into two 12×4-inch rectangles; firmly press perforations to seal. Brush dough with melted butter; sprinkle with brown sugar mixture.

**3.** Starting with long side, roll up tightly jelly-roll style; pinch seams to seal. Cut each roll crosswise into 12 (1-inch) slices with serrated knife; place slices cut sides up about 1½ inches apart on prepared baking sheet.

**4.** Bake about 10 minutes or until golden brown. Remove to wire rack to cool slightly.

**5.** Combine powdered sugar and 1 tablespoon milk in small bowl; whisk until smooth. Add additional milk, if necessary, to reach desired glaze consistency. Drizzle glaze over buns.

# Reuben Rolls

MAKES 8 ROLLS

1 cup sauerkraut

1 package (about 14 ounces) refrigerated
pizza dough

6 thin slices Swiss cheese (about 4 ounces)

1 teaspoon caraway seeds

½ teaspoon black pepper

⅓ pound thinly sliced corned beef

½ cup Thousand Island dressing

**1.** Preheat oven to 400°F. Line baking sheet with parchment paper. Squeeze sauerkraut as dry as possible to yield about ⅔ cup.

**2.** Unroll dough on clean work surface or cutting board; press into 13×9-inch rectangle. Arrange cheese slices over dough, leaving 1 inch border on all sides. Sprinkle with sauerkraut, caraway seeds and pepper. Top with corned beef.

**3.** Starting with long side, gently roll up dough jelly-roll style. Trim off ends. Cut crosswise into eight ½-inch slices with serrated knife; place slices cut sides up on prepared baking sheet.

**4.** Bake 20 to 25 minutes or until cheese is melted and rolls are golden brown. Immediately remove from baking sheet; serve warm with dressing for dipping.

# Twists

## & TURNS

## Herb Cheese Twists

### MAKES 10 TWISTS

2 tablespoons butter

¼ cup grated Parmesan cheese

1 teaspoon dried parsley flakes

1 teaspoon dried basil

1 package (6 ounces) refrigerated buttermilk biscuits (5 biscuits)

**1.** Preheat oven to 400°F. Line baking sheet with parchment paper or spray with nonstick cooking spray.

**2.** Place butter in small microwavable bowl; microwave on MEDIUM (50%) 1 minute or just until melted. Cool slightly; stir in cheese, parsley and basil.

**3.** Separate biscuits; stretch each biscuit into 5×2-inch rectangle. Spread 1 teaspoon butter mixture on each rectangle. Cut in half lengthwise; twist three or four times. Place on prepared baking sheet.

**4.** Bake 8 to 10 minutes or until golden brown. Serve warm.

**VARIATION:** Save even more time by using ready-to-bake breadsticks. Spread the butter mixture on the breadsticks, then bake according to the package directions.

# Pizza Turnovers

## MAKES 6 SERVINGS

6 ounces bulk Italian turkey sausage

½ cup pizza sauce

1 package (about 14 ounces) refrigerated pizza dough

⅓ cup shredded Italian cheese blend

1. Preheat oven to 425°F. Line baking sheet with parchment paper or spray with nonstick cooking spray.

2. Brown sausage in medium skillet over medium heat, stirring to break up meat. Drain fat. Add pizza sauce; cook and stir until heated through.

3. Unroll pizza dough on prepared baking sheet; pat into 12×8-inch rectangle. Cut into six 4-inch squares. Divide sausage mixture evenly among squares. Sprinkle with cheese. Fold dough over filling to form triangles. Press edges with fork to seal.

4. Bake 11 to 13 minutes or until golden brown. Serve warm or cool on wire rack and freeze.

∞ TIP: To freeze turnovers, remove to wire rack to cool 30 minutes. Individually wrap in plastic wrap; place in freezer container or resealable freezer bag and freeze. To reheat turnovers, preheat oven to 400°F. Place in ungreased baking pan; cover loosely with foil. Bake 18 to 22 minutes or until heated through. Or, place one turnover on a paper towel-lined microwavable plate. Microwave on LOW (30%) 3 to 3½ minutes or until heated through, turning once.

# Pesto-Parmesan Twists >

### MAKES 24 BREADSTICKS

1 loaf (1 pound) frozen bread dough, thawed according to package directions

¼ cup prepared pesto

⅔ cup grated Parmesan cheese, divided

1 tablespoon olive oil

**1.** Line baking sheets with parchment paper.

**2.** Roll out dough into 20×10-inch rectangle on lightly floured surface. Spread pesto evenly over half of dough; sprinkle with ⅓ cup cheese. Fold remaining half of dough over filling, forming 10-inch square.

**3.** Roll square into 12×10-inch rectangle. Cut into 12 (1-inch) strips with sharp knife. Cut strips in half crosswise to form 24 strips total.

**4.** Twist each strip several times; place on prepared baking sheets. Cover and let rise in warm place 20 minutes. Preheat oven to 350°F.  Brush breadsticks with oil; sprinkle with remaining ⅓ cup cheese.

**5.** Bake 16 to 18 minutes or until golden brown. Serve warm.

# Olive Twists

### MAKES 12 TWISTS

1 package (11 ounces) refrigerated breadstick dough (12 breadsticks)

1 egg white, beaten

12 pimiento-stuffed green olives, chopped

Paprika

**1.** Preheat oven to 375°F. Line baking sheet with parchment paper.

**2.** Separate dough into individual breadsticks. Brush dough lightly with egg white; sprinkle with olives and paprika. Twist each breadstick three or four times; place on prepared baking sheet.

**3.** Bake 11 to 13 minutes or until golden brown. Serve warm.

# Peanutty Ham Calzone

### MAKES 8 SERVINGS

8 ounces finely diced cooked ham (about 2 cups)

1 cup (4 ounces) shredded Monterey Jack cheese

¼ cup chopped roasted salted peanuts

3 tablespoons orange marmalade

2 tablespoons dried currants

1 to 1¼ teaspoons medium-hot chili powder

1 package (16 ounces) refrigerated jumbo buttermilk biscuits (8 biscuits)

**1.** Preheat oven to 350°F. Line baking sheet with parchment paper.

**2.** Combine ham, cheese, peanuts, marmalade, currants and chili powder to taste in medium bowl; mix well.

**3.** Separate biscuits; roll out each biscuit into 6-inch circle on lightly floured surface. Spoon about ⅓ cup filling into center of each biscuit. Fold dough over filling to form semicircle; press edges to seal tightly. Crimp edges, if desired. Place on prepared baking sheet.

**4.** Bake 15 minutes or until golden brown and filling is heated through. Serve warm or at room temperature.

---

 TIP: Calzones can be refrigerated for up to two days or frozen up to one month.

# Mini Dizzy Dogs >

## MAKES 20 APPETIZERS

½ sheet refrigerated crescent roll dough
(half of 8-ounce package)

20 mini hot dogs or smoked sausages
Ketchup and mustard

**1.** Preheat oven to 375°F. Line baking sheet with parchment paper.

**2.** Cut dough lengthwise into 20 (¼-inch) strips. Coil one dough strip around one hot dog. Place on prepared baking sheet. Repeat with remaining dough strips and hot dogs.

**3.** Bake 10 to 12 minutes or until light golden brown. Serve warm with ketchup and mustard for dipping.

# Stromboli Sticks

## MAKES 10 STICKS

1 package (13.8 ounces) refrigerated
pizza dough
10 mozzarella cheese sticks

30 thin slices pepperoni
1 jar (1 pound 8 ounces) RAGÚ® Old World
Style® Pasta Sauce, heated

**1.** Preheat oven to 425°F. Grease baking sheet; set aside.

**2.** Roll pizza dough into 13×10-inch rectangle. Cut in half crosswise, then cut each half into 5 strips.

**3.** Arrange 1 cheese stick on each strip of pizza dough, then top with 3 slices pepperoni. Fold edges over, sealing tightly.

**4.** Arrange stromboli sticks on prepared baking sheet, seam side down. Bake 15 minutes or until golden. Serve with Pasta Sauce for dipping.

**PREP TIME:** 15 minutes
**COOK TIME:** 15 minutes

# Ham, Apple and Cheese Turnovers

## MAKES 6 TURNOVERS

1¼ cups chopped cooked ham

¾ cup finely chopped peeled apple

¾ cup (3 ounces) shredded Cheddar cheese

1 tablespoon brown mustard

1 package (about 14 ounces) refrigerated pizza dough

1. Preheat oven to 400°F. Line baking sheet with parchment paper or spray with nonstick cooking spray.

2. Combine ham, apple, cheese and mustard in medium bowl; mix well.

3. Roll out dough into 15×10-inch rectangle on lightly floured surface. Cut into six 5-inch squares. Divide ham mixture evenly among squares. Moisten edges with water; fold dough over filling to form triangles. Press edges with fork to seal. Place on prepared baking sheet. Prick tops of each turnover with fork.

4. Bake about 15 minutes or until golden brown. Serve warm or cool 1 hour on wire rack.

# Cheesy Heart Breadsticks

## MAKES 8 BREADSTICKS

1 teaspoon Italian seasoning

¼ teaspoon red pepper flakes

1 loaf (1 pound) frozen bread dough, thawed according to package directions

2 tablespoons olive oil

1 cup (4 ounces) shredded Italian cheese blend

**1.** Preheat oven to 375°F. Line two baking sheets with parchment paper. Combine Italian seasoning and red pepper flakes in small bowl.

**2.** Divide dough into eight pieces. Working with one piece at a time, roll dough into 14-inch rope. Shape ropes into hearts on prepared baking sheets; pinch ends together to seal.

**3.** Brush hearts with oil; sprinkle evenly with seasoning mixture. Sprinkle with cheese, pressing to adhere.

**4.** Bake 18 minutes or until golden brown and cheese is melted. Serve warm.

∞ TIP: Be sure to plan ahead and allow time for the dough to thaw. Frozen bread dough takes 2 to 3 hours to thaw at room temperature. Or the dough may be placed in the refrigerator overnight; it will take 10 to 12 hours to thaw in the refrigerator.

# Spicy Beef Turnovers

### MAKES 10 APPETIZERS

8 ounces ground beef or turkey

2 cloves garlic, minced

2 tablespoons soy sauce

1 tablespoon water

½ teaspoon cornstarch

1 teaspoon curry powder

¼ teaspoon Chinese five-spice powder*

¼ teaspoon red pepper flakes

2 tablespoons minced green onion

1 package (7½ ounces) refrigerated buttermilk biscuits (10 biscuits)

1 egg

1 tablespoon water

*Chinese five-spice powder consists of cinnamon, cloves, fennel seed, star anise and Szechuan peppercorns. It can be found at Asian markets and in most supermarkets.*

**1.** Preheat oven to 400°F. Line baking sheet with parchment paper or spray with nonstick cooking spray.

**2.** Cook beef and garlic in medium skillet over medium-high heat until beef is no longer pink, stirring to break up meat. Drain fat.

**3.** Whisk soy sauce and water into cornstarch in small bowl until smooth. Add soy sauce mixture, curry powder, five-spice powder and red pepper flakes to skillet; cook and stir 30 seconds or until liquid is absorbed. Remove from heat; stir in green onion.

**4.** Separate biscuits; roll out each biscuit into 4-inch circle between two sheets of waxed paper. Spoon heaping tablespoon beef mixture onto one side of each biscuit; fold dough over filling to form semicircle. Pinch edges together to seal. Place turnovers on prepared baking sheet. Beat egg and water in small bowl; brush lightly over turnovers.

**5.** Bake 9 to 10 minutes or until golden brown. Serve warm or at room temperature.

⚭ TIP: The turnovers may be wrapped before baking and frozen up to three months. Thaw completely before baking as directed in step 5.

# Ham and Swiss Twists

## MAKES ABOUT 22 TWISTS

1 package (about 14 ounces) refrigerated pizza dough

6 very thin slices Swiss cheese

6 very thin slices smoked ham

Black pepper

**1.** Preheat oven to 400°F. Line baking sheets with parchment paper.

**2.** Unroll dough on cutting board; press into 16×12-inch rectangle. Arrange single layer of cheese slices over half of dough, cutting slices to fit as necessary. Top with ham slices; sprinkle with pepper. Fold remaining half of dough over ham and cheese layers to form 12×8-inch rectangle.

**3.** Cut dough into ½-inch strips (8 inches long). Twist strips several times; place on prepared baking sheets.

**4.** Bake about 14 minutes or until golden brown. Serve warm.

**TIP:** For added flavor, spread honey or Dijon mustard over dough before layering with cheese and ham. Serve with additional mustard for dipping.

**NOTE:** Ham and Swiss Twists are about 12 inches long. For smaller twists, cut in half after baking.

# Speedy Salami Spirals >

## MAKES ABOUT 28 SPIRALS

1 package (about 14 ounces) refrigerated pizza dough

1 cup (4 ounces) shredded Italian cheese blend
3 to 4 ounces thinly sliced Genoa salami

**1.** Preheat oven to 400°F. Line large baking sheet with parchment paper or spray with nonstick cooking spray.

**2.** Unroll dough on cutting board or clean work surface; press into 15×10-inch rectangle. Sprinkle evenly with cheese; top with salami.

**3.** Starting with long side, roll up tightly jelly-roll style; pinch seam to seal. Cut crosswise into ½-inch slices; place slices cut sides up on prepared baking sheet. (If roll is too soft to cut, refrigerate or freeze until firm.)

**4.** Bake about 15 minutes or until golden brown. Serve warm.

# Sugar and Spice Twists

## MAKES 12 TWISTS

2 tablespoons granulated sugar
½ teaspoon ground cinnamon

1 package (11 ounces) refrigerated breadstick dough (12 breadsticks)

**1.** Preheat oven to 350°F. Line baking sheet with parchment paper or spray with nonstick cooking spray.

**2.** Combine sugar and cinnamon in large shallow dish. Separate breadsticks; roll each piece into 12-inch rope. Roll ropes in cinnamon-sugar to coat.

**3.** Twist each rope into pretzel shape. Place on prepared baking sheet.

**4.** Bake 15 to 18 minutes or until lightly browned. Remove to wire rack to cool 5 minutes. Serve warm.

**TIP:** Use colored sugar sprinkles in place of the granulated sugar in this recipe for a fun "twist" of color perfect for holidays, birthdays or simple everyday celebrations.

# Antipasto Biscuit Sticks

## MAKES 8 BISCUIT STICKS

2 cups biscuit baking mix

½ teaspoon crushed dried oregano

2 tablespoons cold butter, cut into thin slices

½ to ⅔ cup milk

¼ cup finely chopped pimiento-stuffed olives

¼ cup finely chopped salami*

¼ cup finely chopped or shredded provolone cheese

*Hard salami is too chewy for these biscuits; use sandwich salami.*

1. Preheat oven to 425°F. Line baking sheet with parchment paper or spray with nonstick cooking spray.

2. Combine biscuit mix and oregano in large bowl. Cut in butter with pastry blender or two knives until mixture resembles coarse crumbs. Gradually stir in enough milk to form slightly sticky dough. Gently knead in olives, salami and cheese.

3. Turn dough out onto lightly floured surface. Pat into rectangle about ¾ inch thick. Cut dough into eight strips with sharp knife; gently roll each strip into rounded breadstick shape. Place 1 inch apart on prepared baking sheet.

4. Bake 11 to 14 minutes or until golden brown. Remove to wire rack to cool.

SERVING SUGGESTION: For a delicious appetizer, serve the biscuit sticks with marinara sauce or extra virgin olive oil for dipping.

# Dough
—∞—
# MAGIC

## Bedrock Fruit Boulders

### MAKES 16 SERVINGS

1 package (16 ounces) refrigerated jumbo
    buttermilk biscuits (8 biscuits)

1¼ cups finely chopped apple (1 small apple)

⅓ cup dried mixed fruit bits

2 tablespoons packed brown sugar

½ teaspoon ground cinnamon

1 cup sifted powdered sugar

4 to 5 teaspoons orange juice

**1.** Preheat oven to 350°F. Line baking sheet with parchment paper or spray lightly with nonstick cooking spray.

**2.** Separate biscuits; cut each biscuit in half horizontally to make 16 rounds. Roll each round into 3½-inch circle.

**3.** Combine apple, dried fruit, brown sugar and cinnamon in small bowl; mix well. Spoon 1 rounded tablespoon apple mixture into center of each circle. Moisten edges of dough with water. Pull dough up and around filling, completely enclosing filling. Pinch edges to seal. Place seam side down on prepared baking sheet.

**4.** Bake 16 to 18 minutes or until golden brown. Cool 10 minutes on wire rack.

**5.** Combine powdered sugar and 4 teaspoons orange juice in small bowl; whisk until smooth. Add addtional orange juice, if necessary, to reach drizzling consistency. Spoon glaze over rolls. Serve warm.

# Sandwich Monsters

## MAKES 7 SANDWICHES

1 package (16 ounces) refrigerated jumbo buttermilk biscuits (8 biscuits)

1 cup (4 ounces) shredded mozzarella cheese

⅓ cup sliced mushrooms

2 ounces pepperoni slices (about 35 slices), quartered

½ cup pizza sauce, plus additional for dipping

1 egg, beaten

1. Preheat oven to 350°F. Line baking sheet with parchment paper.

2. Separate biscuits; set aside one biscuit for decorations. Roll out remaining biscuits into 7-inch circles on lightly floured surface.

3. Top half of each circle evenly with cheese, mushrooms, pepperoni and sauce, leaving ½-inch border. Fold dough over filling to form semicircle; seal edges with fork. Brush tops with egg.

4. Split remaining biscuit horizontally and cut each half into eight ¼-inch strips. For each sandwich, roll two strips of dough into spirals to create eyes. Divide remaining two strips of dough into seven pieces to create noses. Arrange eyes and noses on tops of sandwiches; brush with egg. Place on prepared baking sheet.

5. Bake 20 to 25 minutes or until golden brown. Remove to wire racks to cool 5 minutes. Serve with additional pizza sauce.

# Chocolate-Stuffed Doughnuts

## MAKES 10 DOUGHNUTS

½ cup semisweet chocolate chips

2 tablespoons whipping cream

1 package (7½ ounces) refrigerated buttermilk
   biscuits (10 biscuits)

½ cup granulated or powdered sugar

¾ cup vegetable oil

**1.** Combine chocolate chips and cream in small microwavable bowl. Microwave on HIGH 20 seconds; stir. Microwave at additional 15-second intervals, if necessary, until chocolate is melted and mixture is smooth. Cover and refrigerate 1 hour or until solid.

**2.** Separate biscuits. Using melon baller or small teaspoon, scoop out 1 rounded teaspoon chocolate mixture; place in center of each biscuit. Press dough up and around chocolate; pinch to form a ball. Roll pinched end on work surface to seal dough and flatten ball slightly.

**3.** Place sugar in shallow dish. Heat oil in small skillet until hot but not smoking. Cook doughnuts in small batches about 30 seconds per side or until golden brown on both sides. Drain on paper towel-lined plate.

**4.** Roll warm doughnuts in sugar to coat. Serve warm or at room temperature. (Doughnuts are best eaten within a few hours of cooking.)

---

&#x221e;   TIP:  For a quicker chocolate filling, use chocolate chips instead of the chocolate-cream mixture. Place six to eight chocolate chips in the center of each biscuit. Proceed with shaping and cooking doughnuts as directed.

# Easy Empanadas

## MAKES 12 EMPANADAS

1 cup prepared refrigerated barbecued
shredded pork

2 tablespoons ORTEGA® Taco Sauce,
any variety

1 tablespoon ORTEGA® Fire-Roasted
Diced Green Chiles

1 can (12 count) refrigerated biscuits

1 egg, well beaten

1 cup ORTEGA® Black Bean & Corn Salsa

**PREHEAT** oven to 375°F. Mix pork, taco sauce and chiles in small bowl.

**SEPARATE** biscuits into 12 pieces. Flatten each biscuit into 6-inch round using rolling pin. Divide filling evenly among biscuits, spreading over half of each round to within ¼ inch of edge. Fold dough over filling; press edges with fork to seal well. Place on ungreased cookie sheet. Brush tops with beaten egg.

**BAKE** 12 to 15 minutes or until edges are golden brown. Immediately remove from cookie sheet. Serve warm with salsa for dipping.

PREP TIME: 10 minutes
START TO FINISH TIME: 25 minutes

# Raspberry White Chocolate Danish

## MAKES 8 SERVINGS

1 package (8 ounces) refrigerated crescent roll dough

8 teaspoons seedless raspberry preserves

1 ounce white chocolate, chopped

1. Preheat oven to 375°F. Line large baking sheet with parchment paper or spray with nonstick cooking spray.

2. Unroll crescent roll dough; separate into eight triangles. Place 1 teaspoon preserves in center of each triangle. Fold right and left corners of long side over filling to top corner to form rectangle. Pinch edges to seal. Place seam side up on prepared baking sheet.

3. Bake 12 minutes or until lightly browned. Remove to wire rack to cool 5 minutes.

4. Place white chocolate in small resealable food storage bag. Microwave on MEDIUM (50%) 1 minute; gently knead bag. Microwave and knead at additional 20-second intervals until chocolate is completely melted. Cut off small corner of bag; drizzle chocolate over danish.

# Punched Pizza Rounds

### MAKES 20 APPETIZERS

1 package (12 ounces) refrigerated flaky
  buttermilk biscuits (10 biscuits)

80 mini pepperoni slices *or* 20 small pepperoni
  slices

8 to 10 pickled jalapeño pepper slices, chopped
  (optional)

1 tablespoon dried basil

½ cup pizza sauce

1½ cups (6 ounces) shredded mozzarella cheese

Shredded Parmesan cheese (optional)

**1.** Preheat oven to 400°F. Spray 20 standard (2½-inch) nonstick muffin cups with nonstick cooking spray.

**2.** Separate biscuits; split each biscuit in half horizontally to make 20 rounds. Place in prepared muffin cups.

**3.** Press 4 mini pepperoni slices into center of each cup. Sprinkle with jalapeños, if desired, and basil. Spread pizza sauce over pepperoni. Sprinkle with mozzarella.

**4.** Bake 8 to 9 minutes or until bottoms of pizzas are golden brown. Sprinkle with Parmesan, if desired. Let stand 1 to 2 minutes before removing from muffin cups. Serve warm.

# Green Chile Rollover Bites

MAKES 32 BITES

1 package (8 ounces) refrigerated crescent dough

1 package (8 ounces) cream cheese, softened, cut into 4 pieces

2 cans (4 ounces each) ORTEGA® Fire-Roasted Diced Green Chiles, well-drained

⅓ cup milk

1 large egg

1⅓ cups dry bread crumbs

1 packet (1.25 ounces) ORTEGA® Taco Seasoning Mix

ORTEGA® Salsa, any variety

**PREHEAT** oven to 400°F. Grease baking pan.

**SEPARATE** dough into 4 (6×3-inch) rectangles on cutting board; press seams closed. Spread 2 ounces (¼ block) cream cheese onto each rectangle. Top each rectangle evenly with 2 ounces (½ can) chiles. Fold rectangles in half lengthwise. Cut each into 8 pieces.

**COMBINE** milk and egg in small bowl; mix well. Combine bread crumbs and seasoning mix in shallow dish. Dip each dough piece into milk mixture, then roll in bread crumb mixture. Place in prepared baking pan.

**BAKE** 18 to 20 minutes or until golden brown. Serve with salsa.

PREP TIME: 15 minutes
START TO FINISH TIME: 35 minutes

# Mini Cheese Dogs

### MAKES 32 MINI CHEESE DOGS

1 package (16 ounces) hot dogs (8 hot dogs)

6 ounces pasteurized process cheese product

2 packages (16 ounces each) refrigerated jumbo flaky homestyle buttermilk biscuits (8 biscuits per package)

**1.** Preheat oven to 350°F. Line baking sheet with parchment paper or spray with nonstick cooking spray.

**2.** Cut each hot dog into 4 pieces. Cut cheese into 32 (1×½-inch) pieces.

**3.** Separate biscuits; cut each biscuit in half. Wrap one piece of hot dog and one piece of cheese in each piece of dough. Place seam side up on prepared baking sheet.

**4.** Bake 15 minutes or until golden brown. Serve warm.

VEGGIE VARIATION: To make this snack vegetarian-friendly, substitute 8 veggie dogs (soy protein links) for the regular hot dogs. Veggie dogs can be found in the produce section and sometimes the freezer section of the supermarket.

# Rosemary Parmesan Biscuit Poppers

## MAKES 24 APPETIZERS

2¼ cups biscuit baking mix

⅔ cup milk

⅓ cup grated Parmesan cheese, divided

1 tablespoon chopped fresh rosemary *or*
   1 teaspoon dried rosemary, crumbled

1 tablespoon grated lemon peel

⅛ teaspoon ground red pepper

3 tablespoons extra virgin olive oil

⅛ to ¼ teaspoon kosher salt or sea salt
   (optional)

**1.** Preheat oven to 450°F. Line large baking sheet with parchment paper or spray with nonstick cooking spray.

**2.** Combine biscuit mix, milk, ¼ cup cheese, rosemary, lemon peel and red pepper in medium bowl; mix well. Drop dough by teaspoonfuls in 1-inch mounds onto prepared baking sheet. Sprinkle with remaining cheese.

**3.** Bake 8 to 10 minutes or until golden brown. Brush biscuits with oil; sprinkle with salt, if desired. Serve immediately.

## Acknowledgments

The publisher would like to thank the companies listed below for the use of their recipes in this publication.

Dole Food Company, Inc.

Ortega®, A Division of B&G Foods North America, Inc.

The Quaker® Oatmeal Kitchens

Reckitt Benckiser LLC.

Unilever

# Metric Conversion Chart

## VOLUME MEASUREMENTS (dry)

$^1\!/_8$ teaspoon = 0.5 mL
$^1\!/_4$ teaspoon = 1 mL
$^1\!/_2$ teaspoon = 2 mL
$^3\!/_4$ teaspoon = 4 mL
1 teaspoon = 5 mL
1 tablespoon = 15 mL
2 tablespoons = 30 mL
$^1\!/_4$ cup = 60 mL
$^1\!/_3$ cup = 75 mL
$^1\!/_2$ cup = 125 mL
$^2\!/_3$ cup = 150 mL
$^3\!/_4$ cup = 175 mL
1 cup = 250 mL
2 cups = 1 pint = 500 mL
3 cups = 750 mL
4 cups = 1 quart = 1 L

## VOLUME MEASUREMENTS (fluid)

1 fluid ounce (2 tablespoons) = 30 mL
4 fluid ounces ($^1\!/_2$ cup) = 125 mL
8 fluid ounces (1 cup) = 250 mL
12 fluid ounces (1$^1\!/_2$ cups) = 375 mL
16 fluid ounces (2 cups) = 500 mL

## WEIGHTS (mass)

$^1\!/_2$ ounce = 15 g
1 ounce = 30 g
3 ounces = 90 g
4 ounces = 120 g
8 ounces = 225 g
10 ounces = 285 g
12 ounces = 360 g
16 ounces = 1 pound = 450 g

## DIMENSIONS

$^1\!/_{16}$ inch = 2 mm
$^1\!/_8$ inch = 3 mm
$^1\!/_4$ inch = 6 mm
$^1\!/_2$ inch = 1.5 cm
$^3\!/_4$ inch = 2 cm
1 inch = 2.5 cm

## OVEN TEMPERATURES

250°F = 120°C
275°F = 140°C
300°F = 150°C
325°F = 160°C
350°F = 180°C
375°F = 190°C
400°F = 200°C
425°F = 220°C
450°F = 230°C

## BAKING PAN SIZES

| Utensil | Size in Inches/Quarts | Metric Volume | Size in Centimeters |
|---|---|---|---|
| Baking or Cake Pan (square or rectangular) | 8×8×2 | 2 L | 20×20×5 |
| | 9×9×2 | 2.5 L | 23×23×5 |
| | 12×8×2 | 3 L | 30×20×5 |
| | 13×9×2 | 3.5 L | 33×23×5 |
| Loaf Pan | 8×4×3 | 1.5 L | 20×10×7 |
| | 9×5×3 | 2 L | 23×13×7 |
| Round Layer Cake Pan | 8×1½ | 1.2 L | 20×4 |
| | 9×1½ | 1.5 L | 23×4 |
| Pie Plate | 8×1¼ | 750 mL | 20×3 |
| | 9×1¼ | 1 L | 23×3 |
| Baking Dish or Casserole | 1 quart | 1 L | — |
| | 1½ quart | 1.5 L | — |
| | 2 quart | 2 L | — |